FAVOURITE
SOMERSET
RECIPES

compiled by
Amanda Persey

with illustrations
by A. R. Quinton

SALMON

Index

Cover pictures *front:* "Carhampton
back: "Bossington"
Title page: "Porlock"

Printed and published by Dorrigo, Manchester, England © Copyright

Apple, Raisin and Cider Teabread

8 oz. self-raising flour   ¼ teaspoon salt
1 level teaspoon mixed spice   4 oz. butter
3 oz. soft brown sugar
3 oz. raisins soaked in 2 tablespoons cider
1 medium cooking apple, peeled, cored and finely chopped
2 medium eggs

GLAZE
2 oz. soft brown sugar   2 tablespoons cider

Set oven to 350°F or Mark 4. Grease a 2 lb. loaf tin. Place the flour, salt and spice into a bowl. Rub the butter into the dry ingredients until the mixture resembles fine breadcrumbs. Stir in the sugar, apple and raisin/cider mixture. Add the eggs and mix well. Put the mixture into the loaf tin and bake for approximately one hour until golden and cooked through when tested with a skewer. Turn out to cool on a wire rack. Boil the glaze ingredients together for 3 or 4 minutes and brush over the warm loaf. Serve sliced, plain or buttered.

Bossington, near Porlock

Porlock Bay Bake

3 oz. butter   1 medium onion, peeled and diced
½ pint dry white wine   1 bay leaf   3 sprigs thyme
3 lb. mussels, from a reliable source, thoroughly scrubbed with 'beards' removed
1½ lb. potatoes, cooked and cut into ¼-½ inch slices
Salt and freshly ground black pepper
2 cloves garlic, peeled and crushed
2 oz. fresh white breadcrumbs
2 oz. Cheddar cheese, finely grated

Set oven to 375°F or Mark 5. Melt 1 oz. butter in a large pan, cook the onion until it is soft and add the wine, bay leaf and thyme and bring to the boil. Add the mussels and cook for 5–10 minutes until the shells open; any which do not open must *not* be used. Remove the mussels from the liquid with a draining spoon and take them out of their shells. Butter a large ovenproof dish and place a layer of potatoes in the bottom. Season with salt and pepper, dot with garlic and add a layer of mussels. Continue with layering, ending with potatoes on top. Strain the mussels liquid over the dish and top with the breadcrumbs and cheese mixed together. Dot with the remaining butter and bake for 20 minutes until bubbling hot and crisp on top. Serve immediately with a fresh green salad.

Ragged Rabbit

At one time rabbit formed a very important part of any country diet.

1 lb. boneless rabbit cut into 1 inch pieces
2 tablespoons flour seasoned with salt and pepper
2 tablespoons sunflower oil   1 oz. butter
2 medium onions, peeled and diced
4 oz. streaky bacon, chopped   ¼ pint chicken or rabbit stock
¼ pint dry cider   1 tablespoon tomato purée
2-3 sprigs fresh thyme   4 oz. button mushrooms

Set oven to 325°F or Mark 3. Toss the rabbit pieces in the seasoned flour. Heat the oil in a frying pan and when hot add the butter. Brown the rabbit pieces a few at a time and transfer to a casserole dish. Add the onions and bacon to the pan and cook gently until the onions are soft. Stir in the remaining seasoned flour and cook for 2–3 minutes. Remove from the heat and add the stock, cider and tomato purée. Return to the heat and stir until boiling. Pour over the rabbit and add the fresh thyme. Cover the casserole and cook for 1 hour; add the mushrooms and cook for a further 30 minutes or until the rabbit is tender. Serve hot with fresh vegetables.

Pear Tart with Walnut Pastry

4-6 pears, depending on size	½ pint water
4 oz. granulated sugar	2 strips lemon zest

WALNUT PASTRY

10 oz. flour	4 oz. ground walnuts
1 teaspoon ground cinnamon	1 oz. caster sugar
5 oz. butter	1 small egg, beaten

Dissolve the sugar in the water, add the lemon zest and boil for 10 minutes. Peel, halve and core the pears, place in the syrup and simmer gently for 15–20 minutes until they are tender. Remove, set aside and cool. For the pastry put the flour and cinnamon into a bowl and rub in the butter until the mixture resembles breadcrumbs. Stir in the walnuts and sugar and bind together with enough egg to make a firm dough. Knead lightly and chill in the refrigerator for 20 minutes. Set oven to 375°F or Mark 5. Divide the pastry in two and use half to line a 9 inch pie dish. Arrange the cold pears over the base and roll out the remaining pastry to make a lid. Seal around the edges and cut a small steam hole in the centre. Cook for 30–40 minutes until the pastry is crisp and golden. Serve warm with cream.

Cheddar Cheese Straws

4 oz. flour   Pinch of salt
½ teaspoon dry mustard powder   2 oz. butter
2 oz. Cheddar cheese, finely grated   1 egg, beaten
Paprika and finely chopped parsley (optional)

Set oven to 400°F or Mark 6. Lightly flour a baking tray. Place the flour, salt and mustard powder into a bowl. Rub in the butter until the mixture resembles breadcrumbs. Stir in the cheese and add enough egg to form a firm dough. Turn out on to a lightly floured surface and knead lightly until smooth. Roll out to a rectangle ¼ inch thick and cut into strips 3 inches by ½ inch. Place on the baking tray and cook for 10–15 minutes until pale golden in colour. Cool on a wire rack. These cheese straws look very attractive if one end is dipped in paprika and the other in very finely chopped parsley when they are cold.

The Lion Rock, Cheddar Gorge

Sage and Apple Jelly

This is a savoury preserve which is delicious served with lamb,
gammon, pork and sausages.

6 lb. cooking apples (windfalls will do)
2 pints of water
4 or 5 good sprigs sage
2 pints of malt vinegar
Granulated sugar: 1 lb. for each pint of strained juice (3–4 lb. for this recipe)

These quantities will make approximately 6lb. of jelly.

Wash the apples and cut into rough chunks; do not peel or core. Place in a preserving pan and pour on 2 pints of water. Add one sprig of sage. Bring to the boil, reduce heat and simmer for about one hour until the apples are pulpy. Add the vinegar; boil rapidly for 5 minutes. Strain the apples through a jelly bag; do not squeeze the bag or the jelly will be cloudy. Measure the liquid and put it back into the cleaned pan. To each pint of juice add 1 lb. of sugar. Dissolve sugar over a low heat, stirring occasionally. Bring to the boil; boil rapidly for about 10 minutes until setting point is reached. Test in the usual way. Cool for 20 minutes. Chop the remaining sage and boil in some water for 30 seconds; strain through a sieve. Remove scum from the jelly, stir in sage and pour into warm jars. Cover and label.

Bridgwater Carnival Pudding

The Carnival takes place around Bonfire Night and is said to be one of the finest in Europe. This is a very easy pudding to make and quite spectacular!

1 x 8 inch round sponge cake
1 x 15 oz. can fruit (raspberries, mixed fruit salad etc), or fresh fruit
17 fluid oz. block vanilla ice cream   1-2 tablespoons sherry or rum
4 egg whites   8 oz. caster sugar

Set oven to 450°F or Mark 8. Put the sponge cake on to a shallow ovenproof dish and moisten slightly with a little fruit juice and the sherry or rum. Put the ice cream on top of the sponge and pile the fruit over it. Put in the freezer. Whisk the egg whites in a large bowl until stiff and then whisk in half the sugar; fold in the remaining sugar. Spread the meringue over the sponge, ice cream and fruit, being careful to cover it completely and ensuring that the meringue reaches right down to the dish. Place immediately into the oven for 2–3 minutes until it just turns brown. Serve immediately. To make the dish even more special, heat 2–3 tablespoons of brandy, light it and pour, flaming, over the meringue as soon as it leaves the oven.

Esplanade and North Hill, Minehead

Ploughman's Pasties

12 oz. shortcrust pastry

FILLING
1 oz. butter
1 medium onion, skinned and finely diced
1 medium potato, peeled, boiled and chopped
3 medium eggs, hard boiled, peeled and chopped
2 oz. Cheddar cheese, grated
½ teaspoon mixed herbs
Salt and pepper

Set oven to 400°F or Mark 6. Roll out the pastry on a floured surface and cut into six rounds approximately 6 inches in diameter. Prepare the filling by melting the butter in a pan and cooking the onion gently until soft and transparent. Cool. Mix together the potato, eggs, cheese, herbs and seasoning and lastly the onion. Divide the filling between the six pastry rounds. Brush the edges of the pastry with beaten egg or water, fold in half and press together firmly to form a good seal. Crimp the edges and brush with beaten egg to glaze. Place on a greased baking tray and cook for approximately 25 minutes until golden in colour. Serve hot or cold.

Cheese and Onion Soup with Mustard Toasts

1 oz. butter   3 medium onions, skinned and finely diced
1 clove garlic, peeled and finely chopped   1 oz. flour
½ teaspoon dry mustard powder   1 pint milk
½ pint chicken stock or ¼ pint stock and ¼ pint white wine
Salt and pepper   4 oz. Cheddar cheese, grated

MUSTARD TOASTS
Thinly sliced bread, toasted on one side only
Butter   Whole grain mustard

To make the soup, melt the butter in a large pan, add the diced onions and garlic. Cook gently for 10–15 minutes until the onions are soft and transparent. Add the flour and mustard and cook for 2–3 minutes. Remove from the heat and gradually add the milk and stock (or stock and wine), stirring all the time. Return to the heat and, stirring continuously, bring to the boil. When the soup thickens reduce the heat and simmer for 5 minutes. Remove from the heat and stir in the cheese. Serve immediately with Mustard Toasts. To make the Mustard Toasts, butter the untoasted side of the bread and spread generously with mustard. Place under a medium grill for a few minutes until crisp and golden. Cut into fingers and serve with the soup.

Sticky Walnut Squares

BASE
6 oz. flour   4 oz. butter   2 oz. caster sugar

TOPPING
2 medium eggs   2 oz. dessicated coconut   6 oz. soft brown sugar
1 oz. self-raising wholemeal flour   4 oz. walnuts, roughly chopped
½ teaspoon vanilla essence   1 teaspoon ground cinnamon

Set oven to 350°F or Mark 4. Prepare the shortbread base either by putting all the ingredients into a food processor and mixing to crumbs or by rubbing the fat into the flour and stirring in the sugar. Press into an 8 inch square tin and bake for 20 minutes. Mix together all the topping ingredients, spread over the shortbread base and return to the oven for a further 20 minutes. Cool in the tin and cut into pieces.

Somerset Strawberry Baskets

½ lb. fresh strawberries   ½ pint double cream

BRANDY-SNAP BASKETS
It is important to measure ingredients accurately for this recipe
2 oz. butter   2 oz. caster sugar
2 oz. golden syrup (warm the tin before measuring to make it easier)
2 oz. flour   ½ level teaspoon ground ginger
Grated rind of half a lemon

Set oven to 350°F or Mark 4. Cover two baking trays with non-stick paper. Melt the butter with the sugar and syrup in a pan over a low heat. Remove from the heat and stir in the flour, ginger and lemon rind. Place small amounts of the mixture about 6 inches apart on to the baking trays to allow plenty of room for spreading. This amount should make about 10 baskets. Bake one tray at a time for about 8–10 minutes until golden and bubbly. Cool for 2 minutes and, lifting with a palette knife, hang each one over an upside-down paper cake case. When cold they will have set in a basket shape and the paper case can be removed. Whip the cream and fold in half the strawberries. Fill each of the baskets and use the remaining strawberries for decoration.

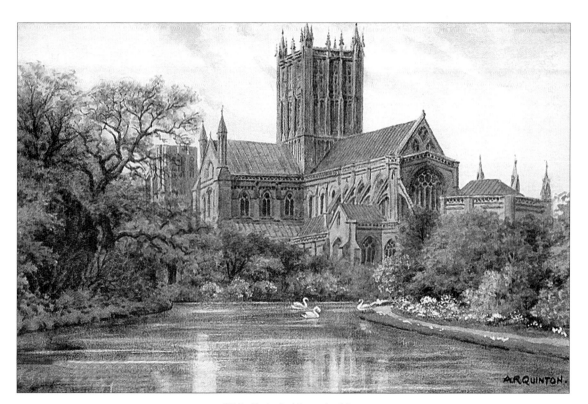

Wells Cathedral from the Moat

Toffee Apples

8 medium-sized eating apples	2 oz. butter
8 wooden skewers	2 teaspoons malt vinegar
1 lb. demerara sugar	¼ pint water
	1 tablespoon golden syrup

Wash the apples and push the skewers into the cores. Prepare the toffee by putting the sugar, butter, vinegar, water and syrup into a large, thick-based pan. Heat gently until the sugar dissolves. Bring to the boil and boil rapidly until the temperature reaches 'soft crack' stage. If you do not have a sugar thermometer, test by dropping a little of the toffee into cold water; it has reached the correct stage when it separates into threads which are hard but not brittle. Dip the apples into the toffee, making sure that they get a good coating. Place on non-stick paper to cool.

Stuffed Pork Chops Baked in Cider

4 x 8 oz. pork chops
½ - ¾ pint dry cider
1 oz. butter for browning the chops

STUFFING
1 oz. butter   1 medium onion, peeled and chopped
1 medium cooking apple, peeled, cored and grated
6 prunes, stoned and chopped   1 oz. walnuts, finely chopped
1 small egg, beaten   4 tablespoons fresh white breadcrumbs
Salt and pepper

Set oven to 425°F or Mark 7. For the stuffing, melt 1 oz. of butter and cook the onion gently until soft. Remove from the heat and add all the remaining stuffing ingredients. Slit the outside edges of the chops to make pockets and push the stuffing into them. Melt the remaining 1 oz. butter in a frying pan and quickly brown each chop. Transfer to an ovenproof dish and pour over about ½ pint of cider; enough to cover the bottom of the dish. Bake for approximately 30–40 minutes until the meat is tender. During cooking, baste the chops from time to time and add more cider if needed. The chops should be served hot with the reduced, syrupy cider liquid poured over them.

The Mendip Hills from Brent Knoll

Mendip Munchies with Tomato Sauce

TOMATO SAUCE

2 tablespoons sunflower or olive oil	1 clove garlic, peeled and crushed
2 medium onions, peeled and diced	½ teaspoon dried mixed herbs
1 carrot, peeled and sliced	1 level teaspoon sugar
1 stick celery, trimmed and sliced	4 tablespoons dry white wine
1–1½ lb. tomatoes, quartered	Salt and pepper

MENDIP MUNCHIES

1 oz. butter   ¼ pint water   2 oz. flour   2 medium eggs, beaten
3 oz. Cheddar cheese, grated   Salt and pepper   Oil for frying

First prepare the sauce. Heat the oil in a large pan and gently cook the onions, carrots and celery for 5 minutes until the onions have begun to soften. Add the tomatoes, garlic, herbs, sugar and wine and simmer gently for 45 minutes. Cool slightly, purée in a food processor and sieve to remove the tomato seeds. Season with salt and pepper. Mendip Munchies: heat the butter and water in a saucepan and when the butter has melted bring to the boil, quickly remove from the heat and add all the flour. Beat well into a smooth paste. Cool slightly and gradually beat in the eggs. Add the cheese and plenty of seasoning. Heat the oil and, when hot, fry teaspoonsful of the mixture until golden brown. Drain on kitchen paper and serve hot with the warm tomato sauce.

Baked Apples with Creamy Custard Sauce

4 large cooking apples   **¼ pint orange juice**

FILLING
8 dried 'no-soak' apricots   1 tablespoon raisins
Grated rind of one orange   1 tablespoon demerara sugar
1 oz. butter for topping

CREAMY CUSTARD SAUCE
2 egg yolks   1 level tablespoon caster sugar
½ pint milk   1 level teaspoon cornflour   1-2 drops vanilla essence

Set oven to 375°F or Mark 5. Wash the apples and cut through the skin around the middle of each one. Remove the core from each and stand upright in an ovenproof dish. Pour the orange juice around them. Mix together the filling ingredients and pack into the apples. Top each apple with a knob of butter. Bake for 45 minutes until the apples are soft. Serve hot. Custard Sauce: whisk together the egg yolks and sugar. Mix a little cold milk with the cornflour to form a smooth paste and stir into the egg mix. Heat the rest of the milk to just below boiling point. Pour the warm milk on to the egg mixture and strain back into the pan. Stir over a very gentle heat until the sauce thickens (it should thinly coat the back of a wooden spoon.) Serve hot or cold with the baked apples.

Taunton Toasts

4 thick slices of a large loaf of bread, white or wholemeal
2 oz. butter   1 level tablespoon dry English mustard
4 tablespoons cider   8 oz. mature Cheddar cheese, grated
Salt and pepper

Melt the butter in a saucepan, being careful not to burn. Stir in the mustard, cider and cheese and continue stirring until the mixture is smooth and creamy and the cheese has just melted. Taste, and season with salt and pepper. Remove the pan from the heat. Toast the bread on both sides and spread the mixture evenly over each slice. Grill until just turning golden and bubbly. Serve immediately.

Market Day Stew with Herby Dumplings

2 tablespoons sunflower oil   1 oz. butter   1½ lb. boneless leg of lamb
2 medium onions, peeled and diced   3 carrots, peeled and cut into sticks
2 sticks celery, cut into 1 inch slices   1 small turnip, peeled and quartered
2 tablespoons flour   1½ pints lamb stock   ½ teaspoon dried mixed herbs
Salt and pepper

DUMPLINGS
4 oz. self-raising flour   2 oz. shredded suet
½ level teaspoon dried ground rosemary
Cold water to mix   Salt and pepper

Cut the meat into 1 inch cubes. Heat the oil in a frying pan, add the butter and brown the meat a little at a time; transfer it to a large saucepan. Add the onions, carrots, celery and turnip to the remaining oil in the frying pan and cook gently until the onions are soft. Stir in the flour and cook for a few minutes; add the stock, herbs and salt and pepper. Pour this over the meat, cover and simmer for 1–1½ hours. Prepare the dumplings by mixing together the flour, suet, herbs, salt and pepper and adding enough cold water to make a soft dough. Shape into 10 small balls and add to the stew and cook for a further 20 minutes until the dumplings are risen and the meat tender. Serve with boiled potatoes and green vegetables.

High Street and Yarn Market, Dunster

Crystal Palace Pudding

Wassailing is an ancient custom carried out on the Twelfth Night to encourage a better harvest from the fruit (particularly apple) trees at which a punch, such as this may be drunk.

4 red eating apples　　　**2 or 3 strips of lemon peel**
2 pints brown ale　　　　**¼ teaspoon ground cinnamon**
½ pint dry sherry　　　　**¼ teaspoon ground nutmeg**
2 oz. soft brown sugar　　**¼ teaspoon ground mixed spice**

Set oven to 350°F or Mark 4. Wash the apples and score a line through the skin around the centre of each one. Place in a casserole dish which can also be used on the cooker hob and add the sugar and ¼ pint of brown ale. Cover and cook in the oven for 30 minutes until the apples are tender. Remove the apples and keep to one side. Add the remaining brown ale, sherry, lemon peel and spices to the casserole dish and simmer for 5 minutes on the hob to allow the flavours to mingle; add the apples and serve hot.

Resurrection Pie

This is a recipe to use up left-over meat from a Sunday roast.

1½ lb. cold meat, minced	½ pint beef stock
2 tablespoons beef dripping	2 level tablespoons tomato purée
2 onions, peeled and diced	½ teaspoon mixed herbs
1 tablespoon flour	2 carrots, peeled and thinly sliced

Salt and pepper

TOPPING

2 lbs. potatoes, peeled and cut into quarters   3 tablespoons milk
1 oz. butter   Salt and pepper   3 oz. Cheddar cheese

Cook the potatoes in boiling salted water for 15–20 minutes until soft. Mash until smooth and mix with the milk and butter, season with salt and pepper. Set oven to 400°F or Mark 6. Prepare the base by melting the beef dripping in a saucepan and gently cooking the onions until soft. Stir in the flour and cook for 2–3 minutes; remove from the heat and add the beef stock. Return to the heat and, stirring, bring to the boil; add the tomato purée, herbs and carrots and simmer gently for 10 minutes. Stir in the meat, season with salt and pepper and cook for a further 10 minutes. Transfer the meat mixture to a shallow ovenproof dish and top with the mashed potatoes and lastly the grated cheese. Bake for 20–25 minutes until the top is well browned.

Winter Gardens and Pavilion, Weston-super-Mare

Somerset Chicken

4 chicken portions   2 oz. butter
1 medium onion, peeled and diced   1 oz. flour
¾ pint milk   ¼ pint dry Somerset cider
4 oz. Cheddar cheese, grated
1 level teaspoon made English mustard
Salt and pepper

Set oven to 350°F or Mark 4. Melt half the butter in a frying pan and lightly brown the chicken pieces. Transfer to a casserole dish and roast for approximately 1 hour until cooked through. Prepare the sauce by melting the remaining 1 oz. butter in a saucepan and gently cooking the onion until soft and transparent. Stir in the flour and cook gently for 2–3 minutes, stirring all the time. Remove the pan from the heat and gradually stir in all the milk and cider. Return to the heat and bring to the boil, stirring all the time until the sauce thickens. Cook for 2–3 minutes. Remove from the heat and stir in three-quarters of the cheese, the mustard and salt and pepper to taste. Pour the sauce over the cooked chicken, sprinkle with the remaining cheese and brown in a hot oven or under a grill. Serve hot with green vegetables and jacket potatoes.

Leek and Curd Cheese Flan

PASTRY
3 oz. white and 3 oz. wholemeal flour
¼ level teaspoon salt   2 oz. butter
1 oz. lard   Cold water

FILLING
2 medium leeks, trimmed and cut into ¼ inch slices
1 oz. butter   4 oz. curd cheese   ¼ pint milk
1 medium egg   1 dessertspoon made English mustard

Set oven to 375°F or Mark 5. Make the shortcrust pastry by the traditional rubbing in method. Rest it in the refrigerator for 30 minutes. Line an 8 inch flan dish with the pastry and bake 'blind' for 10 minutes. Prepare the filling by cooking the leeks gently in the butter for 5 minutes until just soft. In a large bowl beat the curd cheese until soft then gradually beat in the milk, egg and seasoning. Spread a thin layer of mustard over the base of the flan and cover with the leeks and finally the cheese mixture. Bake for approximately 30 minutes until set and pale golden brown.

Aunty Dorothy's Plum Large

3 lb. large, ripe Victoria plums   3 lb. preserving sugar
¾ pint water

Makes approximately 5 lb. of jam

Wash the plums, cut each in half and remove the stones. Crack the stones, remove the kernels and keep to one side. Put the plums and water into a thick-based pan and cook gently until the plums are really soft, about 30 minutes. Add the sugar, stir until it dissolves and add the kernels. Bring to the boil and continue boiling rapidly until setting point is reached. If using a sugar thermometer a set will be obtained when the temperature reaches 221°F. Alternatively, test on a cold saucer; when the jam wrinkles it is set. Remove the pan from the heat and leave to stand for 15 minutes; this will prevent the fruit from rising to the top when it is potted. Pour the jam into clean, warm jars and cover and seal.

Bath Buns

1 lb. strong white flour	4 oz. sultanas
½ teaspoon salt	2 oz. chopped mixed peel
2 oz. butter	1 oz. fresh yeast
2 oz. caster sugar	½ pint tepid milk

2 medium eggs, beaten

TOPPING
2 oz. coarse sugar   1 beaten egg

Put the flour and salt into a large bowl and rub in the butter. Stir in the sugar, sultanas and mixed peel. Blend the yeast with a little of the tepid milk to a smooth cream. Make a well in the centre of the flour and add the yeast liquid, the beaten eggs and remaining milk and mix to a soft dough. Knead on a lightly floured surface until smooth. Place in a clean bowl, cover with a damp cloth and leave to rise in a warm place until double in size. Reknead the dough and divide into 16 even-size pieces. Shape into rounds and place, well spaced, on to greased baking trays. Cover with a damp cloth and leave to prove in a warm place until double in size. Brush with egg and sprinkle with coarse sugar. Bake in a preheated oven 375°F or Mark 5 for 20 minutes until golden. Cool on a wire rack and serve buttered.

Pulteney Bridge, Bath

Hot Beetroot with Orange Dressing

This simple and unusual way of serving beetroot is an excellent accompaniment to many meats, particularly gammon.

3-4 medium-sized beetroots   **1 oz. butter**
Rind and juice of one orange   **Salt and pepper**

Gently wash the beetroots and twist off the leaves above the root so that the skin is not broken. This is to prevent the beetroot bleeding and consequent loss of colour and flavour. Boil in hot water for approximately 1½ hours depending on the size of the roots adding salt and pepper to taste. Run the beetroot under cold water and slip off the skin using your hands; it will come away very easily. Dice the beetroot. Melt the butter in a large pan and add the rind and juice of the orange. Add the beetroot and toss well in the orange mixture. Serve hot.

Poached Pears with Butterscotch Sauce

8 pears   4 oz. granulated sugar   ½ pint water

BUTTERSCOTCH SAUCE
4 oz. butter   3 oz. soft brown sugar
1 oz. golden syrup   ¼ pint double cream

Prepare a sugar syrup by dissolving the granulated sugar in the water and then boiling for 5 minutes. Peel, halve and core the pears and put into the hot syrup. Cover and poach for 10–15 minutes. When the pears are tender leave in the syrup until quite cold. (The syrup may be used in a fruit salad.) Butterscotch Sauce: Put the butter, sugar, golden syrup and cream into a heavy-based pan and heat gently until the butter has melted and sugar dissolved. Increase the heat and boil steadily for 5 minutes. Serve warm or cold with the pears. This sauce is also delicious served with ice cream. Many Somerset gardens have wonderful old pear trees, producing rather firm, but tasty fruit. This is a delicious way of serving them. The softer type of pear does not need poaching.

Exmoor cottage at Selworthy

Exmoor Casserole

2 tablespoons sunflower oil   2 oz. butter
2 lb. venison suitable for casseroling, cut into 1 inch cubes
2 medium onions, peeled and diced
2 cloves garlic, peeled and crushed
2 tablespoons flour   1 pint beef stock
¼ pint port wine   8 oz. black cherries, stoned
1 bay leaf   Salt and freshly ground black pepper

Set oven to 350°F or Mark 4. Heat the oil in a large frying pan and add the butter. Fry the venison a little at a time until well browned and transfer to a large casserole dish. Add the onions to the remaining oil and cook gently until soft, add the garlic and cook for 2–3 minutes. Stir in the flour and cook for 2–3 minutes. Add the stock and the port, stirring all the time and bring to the boil. Stir in the cherries, bay leaf and seasoning and pour this mixture over the meat. Cover the casserole and cook for 1½ to 2 hours until the meat is tender. Remove the bay leaf before serving hot with fresh vegetables. This dish has a better flavour if made the day before it is required and then reheated.

Venison is low in fat and therefore casseroling is an excellent moist method of cooking it.

Potted Meat

This is really a terrine and can be served as a starter with hot toast or as a picnic food with salad. It is best made one or two days before it is served.

8 oz. streaky bacon, derinded (in thin rashers)
1 lb. pork sausagemeat   1 lb. lambs liver
1 medium onion, skinned and diced   1 tablespoon brandy
Salt and pepper
1 level tablespoon freshly chopped herbs; parsley, sage and thyme

Set oven to 350°F or Mark 4. Line a 2 lb. loaf tin with greaseproof paper and then lay the bacon rashers in rows over the bottom and up the sides of the tin. Place the sausagemeat, liver, onion, brandy, salt, pepper and herbs into a food processor and blend the ingredients thoroughly. Alternatively, mince the ingredients and mix well. Place the mixture on top of the bacon and spread evenly. Cover with greaseproof paper and seal with a layer of foil. Stand the loaf tin in a roasting tin half filled with water. Bake in the oven for 1½ hours. Place the terrine, still in its loaf tin, in a cool place and weighed down with heavy weights. When cold, remove the weights and refrigerate until required.

Grilled Herrings with Mustard Sauce

4 fresh herrings, gutted, scaled and washed
Olive oil

MUSTARD SAUCE
½ oz. butter   ½ oz. flour
2 teaspoons English mustard powder
½ pint milk   Juice ½ lemon
1 tablespoon parsley, finely chopped

Mustard Sauce: melt the butter in a saucepan and add the flour; cook for 2–3 minutes, stirring. Remove from the heat, add the mustard powder and gradually stir in the milk. Return to the heat and bring to the boil, stirring all the time. Add the lemon juice and parsley. Set aside and keep warm while the fish is being cooked. Slash the herrings through the skin 2 or 3 times on either side and brush with olive oil. Heat a grill until very hot and cook the herrings for 3–4 minutes on each side until golden and cooked through. Serve hot with the sauce.

Glastonbury Pudding

SPONGE
4 oz. butter   4 oz. caster sugar   2 medium eggs
6 oz. wholemeal self-raising flour
Rind of half a lemon, finely grated

FILLING
1 medium cooking apple, peeled, cored and coarsely grated
3 oz. 'no-soak' dried apricots, finely chopped
3 tablespoons apricot jam
Juice of half a lemon

Grease a 1½ pint pudding basin. Prepare the sponge mixture either by the traditional creaming method and flavouring with the lemon rind or by putting all the ingredients into a food processor and mixing for 30 seconds. Mix together all the filling ingredients. Place a layer of sponge mixture into the base of the pudding basin and top with some of the filling. Continue alternating the layers and finish with a layer of sponge mixture. Cover with a circle of greaseproof paper and then cover and seal with kitchen foil. Steam for 2 hours, topping up the water level from time to time. Remove coverings and leave the pudding in the basin for 5 minutes before turning out onto a warm serving dish. Serve hot with custard or cream.

The Abbey Ruins, Glastonbury

Apple Cheese

This is a preserve with a texture rather like that of lemon curd. It is delicious spread thickly on to fresh bread and is also useful as an unusual filling for a sponge cake.

**2 lb. cooking apples, peeled, cored and sliced
The juice of one lemon   12 oz. granulated sugar
2 medium eggs   4 oz. butter**

These quantities make approximately 3 lb. of 'cheese'

Place the apples and lemon juice into a thick-based pan with just enough water to prevent them burning. Cover and cook until pulped down. Rub the apple pulp through a sieve with a wooden spoon. Return to the pan and add the sugar, eggs and butter and cook very gently, stirring all the time until the mixture thickens. Do not boil. It should be so thick that when the spoon is drawn across the bottom of the pan it leaves a clean line. Pot into clean, warm jars, cover and label.

Cream of Broad Bean Soup

2 oz. butter
2 medium onions, peeled and diced
2 lb. shelled broad beans
1 tablespoon caster sugar

2 pints chicken stock
¼ pint dry white wine or dry sherry
3-4 sage leaves
Salt and pepper

Melt the butter in a large pan and add the onions, broad beans and sugar. Cover and cook gently for 10 minutes, stirring occasionally until the onions are soft. Add the stock, sage leaves and wine or sherry. Simmer for 30–40 minutes until the beans are tender. Cool slightly and purée in a food processor or liquidizer. If a very smooth texture is required the soup may be sieved after liquidizing. Return the soup to the pan, taste and season with salt and freshly ground black pepper.

The Lake and Salthouse Point, Clevedon

Savoury Walnut Plait

This wholesome, nutty bread is delicious served warm with many vegetable soups
or on its own with a thick layer of butter.

2 oz. butter	1 oz. fresh yeast
1½ lb. strong wheatmeal flour	¾ pint tepid water
1 level teaspoon salt	1 teaspoon caster sugar
4 oz. walnuts, roughly chopped	Beaten egg to glaze

Rub the butter into the flour and stir in the salt and walnuts. Blend the yeast with ½ pint of the water and stir in the sugar. Make a well in the flour, add the yeast liquid and enough of the remaining water to make a soft dough. Turn on to a floured surface and knead for 5 minutes until elastic. Cover with a cloth and leave to rise in a warm place until double in size. Knead again and roll into an oblong about 15 inches by 4½ inches. Cut into 3 equal strips, join at the top and plait, dampen the ends and push well together. Transfer to a floured baking tray, cover and leave in a warm place until double in size. Set oven to 425°F or Mark 7. Brush with egg and bake for 30 minutes; reduce heat to 350°F or Mark 4 and cook for a further 15–20 minutes until the loaf sounds hollow when tapped on the base. Cool on a wire rack.

Cheese and Potato Bake

This is a good accompaniment to many meat dishes,
and is also useful as a light supper dish.

2-4 oz. butter
6 medium potatoes, peeled and cut into thin slices
2 medium onions, peeled and thinly sliced
2 cloves garlic, peeled and crushed
4 oz. Cheddar cheese, grated
1 pint full cream milk
Salt and pepper

Set oven to 325°F or Mark 3. Butter a large, shallow ovenproof dish and arrange a layer of potatoes over the base. Add thinly sliced onions, dot with butter, sprinkle over salt, black pepper, a little crushed garlic and about one quarter of the cheese. Continue making layers like this, finishing with a layer of potatoes topped with cheese. Pour on the milk and cover the dish with foil. Cook for 1¼ hours; remove the foil and cook for a further 30 minutes until the potatoes are tender.

Cherry and Almond Flan

8 oz. shortcrust pastry   4 tablespoons cherry or strawberry jam
8 oz. fresh black cherries, washed, stoned and halved (tinned may be used if out of season)
3 medium eggs   4 oz. caster sugar
3 oz. butter, melted and cooled, but not solidified
4 oz. ground almonds   ¼ teaspoon natural almond essence
1 oz. flaked almonds

Roll out the pastry and use to line a 9 inch flan ring. Chill in the refrigerator for 20 minutes. Set oven to 400°F or Mark 6. Spread the jam evenly over the base of the pastry and arrange the cherries over this. If using tinned cherries, drain well. Whisk the eggs and sugar together in a large bowl until they are thick and pale in colour. Fold in the melted butter with a large metal spoon and then the ground almonds and almond essence. Pour this mixture over the cherries and cook for 15 minutes until just beginning to turn brown. Sprinkle on the almonds, reduce oven to 350°F or Mark 4 and continue cooking for a further 20–30 minutes until just set and pale golden brown. Serve warm or cold.

METRIC CONVERSIONS

The weights, measures and oven temperatures used in the preceding recipes can be easily converted to their metric equivalents. The conversions listed below are only approximate, having been rounded up or down as may be appropriate.

Weights

Avoirdupois	Metric
1 oz.	just under 30 grams
4 oz. (¼ lb.)	app. 115 grams
8 oz. (½ lb.)	app. 230 grams
1 lb.	454 grams

Liquid Measures

Imperial	Metric
1 tablespoon (liquid only)	20 millilitres
1 fl. oz.	app. 30 millilitres
1 gill (¼ pt.)	app. 145 millilitres
½ pt.	app. 285 millilitres
1 pt.	app. 570 millilitres
1 qt.	app. 1.140 litres

Oven Temperatures

	°Fahrenheit	Gas Mark	°Celsius
Slow	300	2	150
	325	3	170
Moderate	350	4	180
	375	5	190
	400	6	200
Hot	425	7	220
	450	8	230
	475	9	240

Flour as specified in these recipes refers to plain flour unless otherwise described.